WRIGHT COUSIN ADVENTURES

#1 Fun Cookbook

*50 Favorite Desserts You'll Love to Make,
Bake, Eat and Share!*

Lisa A. Smith
& Gregory O. Smith

Dedication

To families around the world who love to share time with one another both in and out of the kitchen. And to those of present and past generations who have shared their recipes with us. *Bless you!*

Special Thanks

Special thanks to our excellent recipe testing editors, Anne Smith, Madeline Smith, and Elizabeth Evenson. We have so appreciated your encouraging, honest, and helpful feedback in making these recipes *the best tasting desserts out there!*

Authors Note

Good food can bring joy to everyone. Think of the sweet smell of gingerbread in the air, watching homemade ice cream churn and billow up out of the ice cream maker, tasting luscious lemon bars at a church potluck, or handing a small basket of homemade chocolate chip cookies to a friend who's going through a rough time. Sharing favorite desserts makes wonderful memories for us all.

Food can bring such a loving "homemade touch." But you're no doubt busy just like us. You also don't want to spend hours on the internet hunting for that "perfect recipe", only to have the recipe be a big flop, wasting your time and your precious ingredients, again. "Arrgh!" as Tim Wright would say.

This cookbook contains 50 time-tested, totally delicious dessert recipes collected from five generations of amazing cooks in our families. Lisa has gathered, experimented, streamlined, updated, and hand-illustrated *each* delicious recipe. Now, with easy-to-follow directions, most of the treats can be made up and enjoyed in 30 minutes or less.

Greg created the Wright Cousin humor, stories, secret codes, and fun activities. He also got to be one of the fortunate taste-testers, along with our grown kids, grandchildren, and our little neighbors who popped in to say 'Hi!'

"Dessert recipes?" says Lisa. "Go for the Mint Grasshopper Pie, it's always a hit!" "For a movie night," Greg adds, "Chewy Caramel Popcorn can't be beat!"

This cookbook is designed for kids AND adults to have fun working together in the kitchen. There are also lined pages for you to insert your own trustworthy, favorite family recipes.

We hope this cookbook can become a fun, helpful, and reliable dessert reference book for you. So throw on an apron! Dive in! Help your friends and family taste the good things in life through your homemade touch. Best wishes from our family to yours,   *Greg and Lisa Smith*

"**Wow, a new kind of *Wright Cousin Adventures* book!**" said Kimberly Wright.

"Yes," said Lindy, "and this time it's adventures in cooking."

"*Cool*," <u>said</u> Robert, "we've got *our* own #1 Fun Cookbook. I say we make some *Chocolate Chip Cookies* right now."

"I vote for the *Homemade Ice Cream*," said Tim.

"I'm in for the *Frosted Buttermilk Brownies*," said Jonathan.

"It'll be fun to dig into these recipes," said Kimberly. "Hey, have you guys noticed all those little gray hats somebody's drawn in our new cookbook?"

"Hats?" Tim replied, looking at his watch and starting to whistle. "Boy, I wonder who could have done that? Hey, I've got to go. Has anybody seen my gray felt tip marker?"

Psssssst! Hi, this is Tim Wright. I have a secret mission for you!

Throughout this book, I've hidden clues to a TOP SECRET RECIPE. Your mission—should you choose to accept it—is to look for each of my gray spy hat  symbols to retrieve a secret word from that page. Beside each spy hat is a special alphabet LETTER, and somewhere on that page is a secret word underlined in gray. Write that secret word on **page 93**, in the space identified by its alphabet letter.

Once you've filled in all the secret words, the TOP SECRET RECIPE will be yours to make and enjoy. Happy searching and may the spy hat be with you!

— T.W.

— TABLE OF CONTENTS —

Important Baking Hints
(Read this before baking)

A. <u>**Mixing:**</u> As a general rule of thumb when making cookies and many other foods, start by using **two separate mixing bowls**: a large bowl for the wet ingredients and a medium bowl for the dry ingredients. (Lisa likes using a 2 qt., high-sided, **glass** mixing bowl for the wet ingredients.)

B. <u>**Softened Butter:**</u> When a recipe calls for **softened** butter, heat the butter in the microwave for 10 seconds. (The butter should be soft to the touch but not melted.)

C. <u>**Greasing Pans:**</u> There are 3 options:
   - **Spray pans** with baking spray, or
   - **Line pans** with culinary parchment, or
   - Use a **pastry brush to brush pans** with a high-smoke-point oil like **safflower oil, light/refined olive oil, or soybean oil.** (Do not grease pans with butter, extra virgin olive oil, coconut oil, or sesame oil. These are known as low-smoke-point oils. They start smoking when heated above 350°F which can disflavor foods.)

D. <u>**Brown Sugar Substitute:**</u> Many recipes in this cookbook consistently use a **brown sugar substitute: 1 Tbl molasses to 1 cup white cane sugar**. (Sugar mixed with molasses is actually the origin of our "brown sugar" of today.) Their tastes are intensified when mixed together last minute. Stored separately, molasses and sugar have long shelf lives and don't harden over time as brown sugar does.

E. <u>**Sifting:**</u> When a recipe calls for **sifting, please do it**. The resulting fine, airy texture of the powder is vital, removing *all lumps*. (A fine mesh strainer, like you use for removing pulp from orange juice, is author Lisa's favorite sifting tool. Fill and tap it gently to easily sift large amounts of flour and powdered sugar.)

Kitchen Safety Rules

1. Always **wash your hands** and **tie back long hair** before working in the kitchen.
2. If you are a youth, always have a favorite **adult** to be your **kitchen buddy** so you can make these fun treats together.
3. Use **oven mitts or potholders** when working with hot pans. Keep your hands protected. Remember what Kimberly Wright says, "No burns or owies allowed."
4. Keep cold ingredients refrigerated until ready to use.
5. **Don't play around with kitchen tools.** Always be careful and work thoughtfully, especially when working with knives, machines, hot items, and ovens.
6. An important rule of thumb regarding recipes: **"Read Twice, then Gather."** Meaning, read the recipe twice and then gather all the ingredients and tools needed before you cook.
7. IMPORTANT: **Please pay close attention to your health. If you are allergic to any of these foods or food ingredients, please do not prepare, bake, or eat them.**

Abbreviations used in this book:

Tbl = Tablespoon

tsp = teaspoon

oz. = ounce

°F = degrees Fahrenheit

min. = minutes

qt. = quart

"So, which of these cookies and treats is your favorite?" Kimberly Wright asked her 14-year-old brother, Tim.

"Well, I kind of like the *Ingredient Suggestions*," Tim replied.

"Sorry, Tim, that's not a cookie," said Kimberly.

"I know, but it's so hard to decide," said Tim. "The *Chocolate Chip Cookies* sound good, the *Gingersnaps* sound good, and then there's the *Oatmeal Cookies*—you know how much I like Oatmeal Cookies—."

"Well, hurry up and decide. I'll help make any of them that you want."

"Great," said Tim with a grin, "let's make them ALL!"

— CLASSIC COOKIES —

"The Secret of the Yummy Cookie!"

- o Ingredient Suggestions
- o Chocolate Chip Cookies
- o Oatmeal Cookies
- o Snowball Cookies
- o Chewy Gingersnap Cookies
- o Softy Lofty Sugar Cookies
- o Buttercream Frosting for Cookies & Cakes
- o Nana's Fluffy Sugar Cookies
- o Gingerbread Cookies
- o Snickerdoodles

**"One small step for man,
One Giant Cookie for mankind!"**

There's always SPACE for Cookies!

Ingredient Suggestions

A. <u>Non-aluminum Baking Powder</u> such as Rumford brand. (We try to avoid using aluminum in food.)

B. <u>Pure Cane Sugar</u> instead of beet sugar. Cane sugar tastes best. It doesn't have a chemical aftertaste.

C. <u>Vanilla Flavoring</u>:
   - Liquid Vanilla: **Molina Mexican Vanilla Blend** is our preferred vanilla, with its rich flavor and extremely low 1.8% alcohol content. (We try to avoid vanilla flavorings with alcohol. Interestingly, "pure vanilla extract" must have 35% alcohol to be approved by the FDA.)
   - Powdered Vanilla: **(Cook's Pure Vanilla Powder) 1 tsp powdered vanilla = 1 tsp liquid vanilla.**

D. <u>Unbleached, enriched flour</u> is our preferred flour. We use *bleached* flour in sugar cookies to keep them white.

E. <u>Chocolate Chips</u>: Ghirardelli brand tastes best but it is often very expensive. (Watch for sales in the Fall.)

F. <u>Butter</u>: We prefer real butter rather than margarine, shortening, or plant-based butter (which is dairy-free margarine). Actual butter provides a better, richer taste.

G. <u>Brown Sugar</u>: **1 Tbl molasses + 1 cup white cane sugar = 1 cup brown sugar.** When a recipe calls for "brown sugar", just mix in the appropriate amounts of molasses and cane sugar instead. You'll be surprised at how the flavor is intensified. Stored separately, molasses and sugar have long shelf lives and don't harden over time like packaged brown sugar does.

H. <u>Cocoa Powder</u>: We've found **Hershey's Cocoa 100% Cacao Natural Unsweetened** powder tastes best.

I. <u>Grandma's Molasses Unsulphured Original</u> (1 gallon).

Chocolate Chip Cookies

(These cookies are wonderful! Even without chips, as "Chocolate Chipless" Cookies—author Greg's ☺ favorite—they're great! Makes about 30 yummy, 3" cookies.)

1 cup butter, softened
1½ cups sugar
1 Tbl molasses*
2 eggs
½ tsp water
1 tsp vanilla
2½ cups flour
1 tsp baking soda
1 tsp salt
12 oz. chocolate chips (1½ to 2 cups)

Directions

1. In a large, 2 qt. mixing bowl, cream together butter, sugar, and molasses for 2 minutes on high speed with electric mixer. On medium speed, mix in eggs, water, and vanilla.
2. In another mixing bowl, whisk together flour, baking soda, and salt.
3. Add the flour mixture into the wet ingredients bowl and beat on medium-low speed until thoroughly combined.
4. Stir in chocolate chips, according to desired amount.
5. Preheat oven to 350°F. Grease 2 baking sheets or line with culinary parchment.
6. Drop rounded 1½" diameter spoonfuls of dough onto baking sheets, leaving 3" of clearance between each cookie.
7. Bake 8-10 minutes or until cookies are lightly browned around edges. Cool on baking sheet until set, then transfer cookies to wire rack. *Enjoy!*

*Note: *Grandma's Molasses Unsulphured Original*

7

Oatmeal Cookies ☺

(A favorite cookie of young and old alike. Surprisingly, they taste even better when they're a day or two old! *Fantastic!* Greg says they're great with raisins! Makes about 36, 2½ " cookies.)

¾ cup butter, softened
1½ cups sugar
1 Tbl molasses*
2 eggs
1 tsp vanilla
1½ cups flour
½ tsp baking soda
½ tsp salt
3 cups rolled oats (not quick oats)

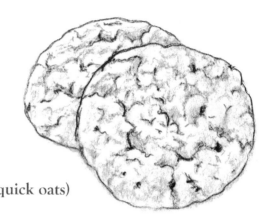

(Optional additions)
1 cup raisins, or
1 cup finely chopped walnuts, or
1 cup chocolate chips

Directions

1. In a high-sided, 2 qt. mixing bowl, cream together butter, sugar, and molasses with electric mixer. Beat in eggs and vanilla.
2. In another 2 qt. mixing bowl, whisk together flour, baking soda, salt, and rolled oats.
3. Add dry ingredients to creamed ingredients. Beat on low speed with electric mixer until fully combined. Stir in optional ingredients, as desired.
4. Preheat oven to 350°F.
5. Drop 1½" spoonfuls of dough onto *ungreased* baking sheet, leaving 2" clearance between drop of dough. (The cookies will spread out to be about 2½" in diameter each.)

6. Bake 8-11 minutes or until cookies are lightly browned around edges. Cool on wire rack. *Enjoy!*

Note: Oatmeal Cookie dough freezes well when shaped as logs and double wrapped in plastic wrap for up to 6 months. When ready to use, remove plastic, cut dough into 5/8" thick slices, and bake on ungreased baking sheets as directed above. *Great!*

*Note: We use *Grandma's Molasses Unsulphured Original* molasses

For fun, try making up a batch of Oatmeal Cookies, half with raisins and the other half with chocolate chips. Which addition do you like best, the ones with chips or the ones with raisins? We'd love to hear your family's vote! *Really!* Let us know at GregoryOSmith.com. It's fun to hear your choice.

Which do YOU like best in your Oatmeal Cookies?

Chocolate Chips?   **Or Raisins?**

Snowball Cookies

(Darling on a dessert tray! These sweet little white cookie balls are also known as Mexican Wedding Cakes or Russian Tea Cakes. They're a festive favorite of both children and adults! Makes about 48, 1" diameter cookie balls.)

1 cup butter, softened
½ cup powdered sugar
1 tsp vanilla
2¼ cups flour
¼ tsp salt
¾ cup finely chopped walnuts
Additional ½ cup powdered sugar (set aside
    in a small bowl to roll cookies in)

Directions

1. In a high-sided 2 qt. mixing bowl, use electric mixer at medium-high speed to cream together butter and ½ cup powdered sugar. Mix in vanilla. On low speed, slowly stir in flour, salt, and finely chopped walnuts until fully combined. Cover bowl with plastic wrap and chill in refrigerator for 15 minutes.
2. Preheat oven to 400°F.
3. Roll dough into 1" balls. Place on ungreased baking sheet, 1" apart from one another.
4. Bake 10-12 minutes or until lightly browned.
5. Roll warm, baked cookie balls around in the set-aside bowl of ½ cup powdered sugar, coating all surfaces.
6. Place cooled Snowball Cookies on a festive dessert tray. *Serve and enjoy!* K

Chewy Gingersnap Cookies

(Soft, sweet and delicious! One of author Greg's favorite
cookies! Makes about 24, 3" diameter cookies)

¾ cup butter
1 cup sugar
¼ cup molasses
1 egg
2 cups flour
½ tsp salt
2 tsp baking soda
1 tsp cinnamon
½ tsp cloves
½ tsp ginger
½ cup sugar (set aside in a bowl)

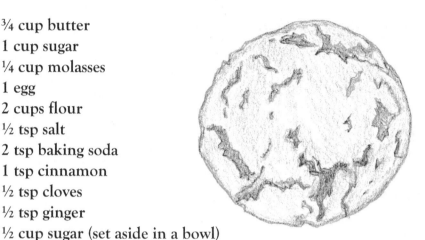

Directions

1. In a large 2 qt. glass mixing bowl, melt butter—with a paper
   towel on top of the bowl so butter won't splatter out— in
   microwave for about 25 seconds. Discard paper towel. Into
   bowl, add 1 cup sugar, molasses, and egg. Beat together with
   electric mixer on medium speed until well combined.
2. In another mixing bowl, whisk together dry ingredients—
   flour, salt, soda, cinnamon, cloves, and ginger. Add dry
   ingredients to butter mixture and beat with electric mixer on
   low speed until completely combined.
3. Cover dough with plastic wrap and chill in fridge until firm.
4. Preheat oven to 370°F. Grease 2 baking sheets.
5. Form dough into 1¼" balls. Roll each ball in the set-aside
   bowl containing ½ cup sugar. Place sugar-coated balls on
   greased baking sheets, 1½" apart.
6. Bake for 8-10 minutes at 370°F. Cool on wire rack. *Yum!*

Softy Lofty Sugar Cookies

(The BEST TASTING rich, soft, puffy sugar cookie topped with frosting and sprinkles! Makes about 38, 3" cookies.)

3½ cups bleached flour, sifted
1/8 tsp salt
1 Tbl baking powder
1 cup butter, softened
1½ cups sugar
2 eggs
¼ cup milk
2 tsp vanilla
(Optional) ¼ tsp almond extract

Directions

1. In a large 2 qt. mixing bowl, whisk together **sifted** flour, salt, and baking powder. (Using sifted flour is important here.)
2. In a high-sided 2 qt. mixing bowl, cream together the softened butter and sugar with an electric mixer at medium-high speed for 3 minutes. (Creaming for 3 minutes is the secret for making these cookies light and fluffy!) Add in eggs, milk, vanilla (and optional almond extract, if using). Mix on medium-low speed until well combined.
3. Gradually pour dry ingredients into wet ingredients and mix on low speed until a soft dough is formed. Cover bowl tightly with plastic wrap and chill in refrigerator for 15 minutes.
4. Preheat oven to 375°F. Grease 2 baking sheets.
5. Retrieve chilled cookie dough and remove covering. Roll dough into 1½" balls with your hands and place on greased baking sheets, 2" apart from each other. Cover loosely with plastic wrap. Flatten balls to be ½" thick by pressing down gently with the bottom of a cup. Remove plastic covering. (This cookie dough may also be rolled out to about 3/8"

thick between two layers of plastic wrap or culinary parchment and cut with cookie cutters.)

6. Bake cookies on middle oven shelf/rack for 8 minutes or until lightly browned around edges.

7. Cool on wire rack. Decorate with **Buttercream Frosting** and candy sprinkles. *So good!*

Buttercream Frosting for Cookies & Cakes

(Tim and Robert Wright like this frosting so much that Kimberly and Lindy have to keep an eye on them so they don't snitch it all!)

½ **cup butter, softened**
3 cups sifted powdered (or confectioner's) sugar
1 tsp vanilla
1 Tbl milk
Food coloring

Directions

1. In a high-sided 2 qt. mixing bowl, cream together the softened butter and sifted powdered sugar with an electric mixer on medium-high speed for 1 minute.

2. Mix in vanilla and milk on low speed. (If you desire a thinner consistency, add more milk, one teaspoon at a time.)

3. Stir in food coloring of your choice and have fun decorating!

Nana's Fluffy Sugar Cookies

(Due to butter and sugar rationing during World War 2, author Lisa's grandmother, Nana, created this lower sugar recipe. It's delicious even today! Makes 30-36, 2" cookies.)

½ cup butter, softened
1 cup sugar
1 egg
½ cup milk
1 tsp vanilla
3 cups flour
¼ tsp salt
1 Tbl baking powder

(Optional Toppings)
Dried fruit pieces, colored sugar crystals, candy sprinkles, or gum drops, or frost with Butter Cream Frosting

Directions

1. In a high-sided 2 qt. mixing bowl, use an electric mixer to cream together the butter and sugar for 3 minutes on medium-high speed. (Creaming for 3 minutes is the secret for adding lightness and volume to these cookies!)
2. At low speed, slowly beat in egg, milk, and vanilla.
3. Sift flour, salt, and baking powder in a separate mixing bowl.
4. Gradually pour the dry ingredients into the wet ingredients while mixing at medium-low speed. Mix until fully combined. Cover dough with plastic wrap and chill in fridge for 15 minutes to let dough stiffen.
5. Roll out dough to 3/8" thickness between 2 layers of plastic wrap or culinary parchment. Remove top layer of plastic wrap or parchment. Cut out shapes with your favorite cookie cutters.

6. With a "pancake turner" spatula, carefully transfer cookie cutouts onto a greased baking sheet leaving ½" clearance around each cookie.

7. Place oven rack/shelf in middle of oven. Preheat oven to 350°F.

8. **(Optional) Nana's World War 2 Secret:** Press dried fruit pieces, colored sugar crystals, candy sprinkles, or gum drops into the top surface of cookies prior to baking. The cookies will come out of the oven pre-decorated and delicious!

9. Bake cookies 8-10 minutes or until they are barely browned around the edges. Remove cookies from oven and let rest 1 minute before transferring to wire rack for cooling.

10. If the cookies were not decorated earlier with candies, they can now be frosted with the yummy **Buttercream Frosting for Cookies & Cakes**. (Two pages back.) *Enjoy!*

Note: Store any extra cookies in a covered container or cookie jar. Cookies can also be frozen for up to 3 months in an air-tight container.

Gingerbread Cookies

(So fun to decorate and to eat! Tim Wright likes to make a whole army of them! Makes about 36, 4" tall cookies.)

½ cup butter, softened
1 cup sugar
1½ cups molasses
1 egg
2/3 cup apple juice
6½-7 cups flour
2 tsp baking soda
1 tsp salt
1 tsp ground cinnamon
1 tsp ground cloves
1 tsp ground ginger
1 tsp ground allspice

Directions

1. In a 3½ qt. mixing bowl, use an electric mixer set at medium-high speed to cream together the butter, sugar, and molasses. At medium-speed, mix in the egg and apple juice.
2. In another large mixing bowl, whisk together 6½ cups flour, baking soda, salt, cinnamon, cloves, ginger, and allspice. Add this dry mixture to the wet mixture and beat at medium-low speed. Slowly beat in more flour, ¼ cup at a time as needed, until dough is no longer sticky.
3. Prepare your table or roll-out surface by slightly dampening it with water. Cover with plastic wrap.
4. Place about 2 cups of dough on the prepared surface. Cover with a top layer of plastic wrap. Using a rolling pin, roll out the dough 3/8" thick. Remove top layer of plastic wrap. Use your favorite cookie cutters to cut out cookies. Set aside excess dough for later.

5. Grease two baking sheets or line with culinary parchment. Transfer cookies to baking sheets, with a pancake turner spatula, leaving 2" space between cookies.
6. Position oven rack in middle of oven. Preheat oven to 350°F.
7. If using raisins for decorating, press them in into the cookies now, prior to baking.
8. Bake cookies on baking sheets in oven for 8 minutes or until cookies are lightly browned around the edges.
9. Remove from oven and cool cookies for 1 minute on their baking sheets. Using a pancake spatula, transfer cookies to wire rack to cool completely.
10. Enjoy **Gingerbread Cookies** with or without frosting! (The **Buttercream Frosting for Cookies & Cakes**—four pages back—works *great!*)

Note: Gingerbread cookie dough freezes well. Roll out cookie dough into 3/8" thick slabs between two layers of plastic wrap. Keeping the dough flat, slip the dough and plastic into a zip freezer bag, and freeze for up to 6 months. Baked gingerbread cookies also freeze well in zip freezer bags for up to 6 months. Having them frozen keeps you ever ready for a wonderful gingerbread cookie decorating and eating party, which author Lisa totally loves!

Snickerdoodles

(Rolled in sugar & cinnamon, these cookies are a favorite!
Makes 32, 2½" delicious cookies)

1 cup butter, softened
1½ cups sugar
2 eggs
2¾ cups flour
¼ tsp baking powder
¼ tsp salt

Set aside in a small bowl:
3 Tbl sugar + 3 tsp cinnamon

Directions

1. In a 2 qt. mixing bowl, use electric mixer to cream together butter, sugar, and eggs at medium-high speed for 2 minutes.
2. In another bowl, whisk together flour, baking powder, salt.
3. Add dry mixture to wet mixture. Beat at medium speed until fully combined.
4. Position oven shelf/rack in middle of oven. Preheat oven to 400°F. Set out 2 ungreased baking sheets.
5. Form dough into 1½" balls. Roll balls in set aside bowl of sugar and cinnamon. Place balls on baking sheets, 2" apart.
6. Bake 8-10 minutes or until cookies are barely set. Remove promptly from baking sheets. Cool on wire rack. *Wonderful!*

Note: This recipe does NOT use the traditional ingredient Cream of Tartar, so it does not have the sour, metallic aftertaste that most Snickerdoodles have.

My Own Cookie Recipes:

Recipe:

Recipe:

Recipe:

Soldier Sam looked out across the muddy battlefield in front of him. "We're going to have to cross that to get to the trenches," he said, tightening his canteen belt.

"It sure looks that way," said soldier Roy. "We'd better call in some artillery support to cover us."

"That, and our air force, too," said soldier Ethan.

"We're out of time. On three, everybody run for our trench," said soldier Joseph. "Three!"

The four soldiers dashed across the muddy bog as fast as they could, but its stickiness began slowing them down. First, soldier Ethan lost a boot, then Roy. Sam almost made it across but suddenly lost both his boots and his socks in the sticky brown goo. Soldier Joseph tried to pull him free.

"Try to keep going!" called out Ethan.

"I can't," replied Roy, "it's got me like quicksand."

"Me too," said Sam. "We're in for it now."

"Timothy Wright," called out Kimberly, just entering the kitchen, "what are your toy soldiers doing in my homemade fudge?"

"Top Secret maneuvers," said Tim, reaching for a spoon and fork. "I'm afraid they're going to have to eat their way out."

— CANDY & POPCORN —

"It's What Movies are Made For!"

- o Peppermint Patties
- o Easy Homemade Fudge
- o Holiday Corn Flake Wreaths
- o Stovetop Popcorn
- o Chewy Caramel Popcorn

Toronto and Kimosoggy strike again!

Peppermint Patties

(Cool! Refreshing! Anne's totally delicious creations!
Makes 50, 1½" patties.)

½ can sweetened condensed milk (or 10 Tbl)
3 drops peppermint oil* or ¾ tsp peppermint extract
3 cups powdered sugar, sifted
2¼ cups semisweet chocolate chips
2 Tbl vegetable oil

Directions

1. Set up electric mixer with a dough or paddle attachment. Combine sweetened condensed milk and peppermint oil in a large mixing bowl. With electric mixer set at medium-low speed, add the sifted powdered sugar into the sweetened milk and peppermint mixture, one cup at a time, until a stiff dough is formed.
2. Cover two baking sheets with culinary parchment or plastic wrap.
3. With your hands, roll dough into 1" balls. Place balls onto covered baking sheets. Flatten each ball into a 1½" disc that is ¼" thick. (Alternative process: Use a rolling pin to roll out dough ¼" thick between two layers of parchment. Remove top parchment. Using a 1½" circle cookie cutter, cut dough into discs. Place discs onto covered baking sheet.)
4. Freeze discs on their covered baking sheets for 30 minutes or up to 24 hours.
5. Once discs are frozen, prepare the chocolate: In a **glass bowl**, melt chocolate chips with vegetable oil in 30 second intervals in the microwave. Stir with a fork between each interval until chocolate and oil are smooth and melted together.

6. Remove discs from freezer. Working with one disc at a time, place the disc in the melted chocolate, using a fork to flip it over quickly, coating all sides. Lift the coated peppermint patty disc out with the fork. If the patty has too much chocolate on it, gently tap the fork on the rim of the bowl to knock some off. Place the patty back onto the covered baking sheet. (If chocolate in the bowl thickens, rewarm it in the microwave to continue working.)

7. Refreeze peppermint patties on their baking sheets until firm to the touch, about 30 minutes. Pull them out of freezer when ready to serve and enjoy.

8. Store any extra peppermint patties in the freezer in a plastic zip bag or airtight container for up to 3 months.

*Note: Our preferred mint flavoring is LorAnn Oils Super-Strength Peppermint Oil. Its flavor is intense, so we only have to use a few drops. (This is a candy flavoring found online and in candy making supply sections in stores.)

Homemade Fudge

(Oh, so good! Easily made with perfection in the microwave.
Fudge is a wonderful gift! Makes about 2 lbs. fudge.)

2 cups chocolate chips (1 cup semisweet + 1 cup milk choc.)
14 oz. can sweetened condensed milk
1 tsp vanilla
10 oz. bag mini marshmallows
(Optional) ½ cup chopped walnuts

Directions

1. Line an 8"x8" pan with culinary parchment or aluminum foil.
2. Combine all ingredients and optional walnuts in a large 2 qt. glass microwave-safe bowl. Microwave for 90 seconds, stopping and stirring every 30 seconds to ensure mixture is thoroughly melted and combined.
3. Pour into lined 8"x 8" pan.* Cool fudge uncovered in the refrigerator for 2 hours.
4. Cut into small squares and serve. (Perfect fudge is a little firm on the outside, but creamy and pillowy on the inside.) Delicious!
5. Store cooled fudge can be stored in an air-tight container for 1 week at room temperature or in the freezer for 3 months. To defrost frozen fudge, pull out of freezer 24 hours ahead of serving time and thaw naturally on the counter.

*Note: You can easily pour the final hot mixture directly into a decorative tin that is lined with culinary parchment. Once fudge is cooled completely, cover with a lid. *This makes a delightful homemade gift!*

Holiday Corn Flake Wreaths

(This treat recipe uses stovetop cooking, no baking required.
Greg especially likes these treats (without the red hots, please!)
Good year-round! Makes 16, 2" diameter wreaths.)

1/3 cup butter
1 pkg (10 oz.) marshmallows
1 tsp green food coloring
6 cups dry corn flakes cereal
Optional for decoration: red cinnamon candies

Directions

1. Cover a baking sheet with culinary parchment or plastic wrap. Grease a large mixing bowl & place corn flakes inside.
2. Melt butter with marshmallows in one of these two ways:
   A. On the stove in a 2 or 3 qt. heavy-bottom saucepan over low heat, stir together until melted. Stir in food coloring. OR
   B. In the microwave, in a 2 qt. microwave-safe bowl, heat butter with marshmallows for 1 minute. Stir down with silicone spatula. Reheat and stir in 15 second intervals until marshmallows fully melt. Stir in food coloring.
3. Pour melted mixture over dry cereal in bowl. Stir together.
4. With buttered hands, quickly pull out 16 small handfuls and place on covered baking sheet. Form them into wreaths.
5. Add optional red cinnamon candies for accents. *Delicious!*

Stovetop Popcorn

(Totally yummy for a family home movie night or for making
Caramel Popcorn! *Enjoy!*)

Popcorn kernels
Vegetable oil
Heavy, thick-based pot & lid
12 qt. giant bowl

Directions

1. Pour vegetable oil into your heavy pot with just enough oil
   to generously cover the bottom surface. Sprinkle in enough
   popcorn kernels to cover the bottom of the pot with a single
   layer of kernels. Gently shake pot to coat popcorn kernels
   with oil. Cover pot with lid.
2. Place pot over medium-high heat on stove. When kernels
   start popping, use oven mitts on your hands and shake the
   pot back-and-forth and side-to-side. Continue shaking until
   popping sounds cease. Remove pot from heat. Take off lid.
3. Still using oven mitts or hot pads, carefully dump the
   popped popcorn into the giant serving bowl. Salt and butter
   to taste. *Enjoy!*

Chewy Caramel Popcorn

(So good, you'll want to eat more than just one soft, chewy bite! Great in a clear gift bag! Makes 4 qts. caramel popcorn.)

4 qts. popped Stovetop Popcorn, unbuttered and unsalted, placed in a large bowl

<u>Caramel Sauce:</u>
1 cup packed brown sugar
½ cup butter
¼ cup light corn syrup
¼ tsp salt
1 tsp vanilla
½ tsp baking soda

Directions
1. In a 2 qt. glass microwave-safe bowl, combine brown sugar, butter, corn syrup and salt. Cover bowl with paper towel to help prevent splatter. Microwave on high, 2 minutes or until mixture is thoroughly melted.
2. Use oven mitts to remove hot bowl from microwave and quickly stir in the vanilla and baking soda with a silicone spatula. The caramel sauce should be bubbly and frothy.
3. Drizzle hot caramel sauce over popped popcorn in large bowl. Stir with silicone spatula to coat all pieces of popcorn.
4. Sprinkle with more salt, if desired. **Chewy Caramel Popcorn** can also be formed into popcorn balls while the caramel is still warm. *Absolutely soooo good!*

Note: To make hardened **Golden Caramel Popcorn** (like *Cracker Jacks*): Refill the 2 qt. microwave-safe bowl with **Chewy Caramel Popcorn**. Microwave it again 1½ min. Spread it loosely onto a greased baking sheet to cool. *Tastes simply amazing!*

My Own Candy Recipes:

Recipe:

_____

_____

_____

_____

_____

_____

_____

_____

_____

_____

_____

_____

_____

_____

_____

_____

_____

_____

_____

_____

_____

Recipe:

"Brownie-in-a-Cup?" said Tim as he and his cousin, Robert, carried several large grocery bags full of cereal in from the car. "Isn't that the recipe from our advanced college chemistry class we attended during our *Wright Disguise* adventure?"

"Yes," said Robert, "it tasted great."

"Hey, I wonder how Kimberly and Lindy are doing with those rice crispy treats they promised us?" said Tim. "They sure make great edible building blocks."

"Yes," said Robert, "remember when we made that cool jungle pyramid out of them for your birthday cake last year?"

"That was fun!" said Tim as they reached the kitchen.

"Hold on, Tim," said Kimberly, glancing at the groceries the boys were carrying, "now that's a lot of cereal. You guys didn't buy the whole store out of rice crispies, did you?"

"No, they've still got one box," Tim replied. "Remember, you said Lindy and you could make enough rice crispy treats for us to build a castle."

"Yes," said Kimberly, "but your toy knights aren't **that** big."

"Who said anything about toy knights?" Tim replied. "We're going to build a castle tower *big enough for us* this time. Robert, hand me the marshmallows. This is going to be fun!"

— BROWNIES & BARS —

"Sweet and Gooey, Rich and Chewy!"

- o Brownie-in-a-Cup
- o Fudgy Brownies
- o Frosted Buttermilk Brownies
- o Rice Crispy Treats
- o Lemon Bars
- o Oatmeal-Berry Bars

"Could this be the top of somebody's future wedding cake?"

Brownie-in-a-Cup

(A quick-fix, personal brownie. Just 45 seconds in the microwave and it's yours! Makes 1 delicious brownie in a 20 oz. cup or mug.)

1½ Tbl butter
3 Tbl sugar
¼ tsp vanilla
pinch of salt
1 egg yolk
4 Tbl flour
1 Tbl cocoa powder
1½ Tbl chocolate chips

Directions

1. Place butter in a 20 oz. microwave-safe cup or mug. Cover mug with a paper towel to prevent butter from splattering. Place covered mug in microwave and heat about 15 seconds until butter is melted.
2. Retrieve mug. Add the sugar, vanilla, salt, and egg yolk to the melted butter. Stir with a fork. Add flour, cocoa powder, and chocolate chips and stir until well combined.
3. Cover mug again with paper towel. Place mug in microwave and cook for 45 seconds. (Microwave cooking times may vary. The finished brownie should be quite moist inside.) *Enjoy every bite!*

Note: If you happen to use a whole egg instead of an egg yolk in this recipe, the ingredients will rise higher in your mug during baking. The finished product will be more cake-like, but it tastes great, too!

Fudgy Brownies

(This is Elizabeth's intense chocolate brownie recipe. Better than a box mix! Serves 24)

½ cup butter, melted
1 cup vegetable oil
4 cups sugar
6 eggs
2 Tbl vanilla
3 cups flour
1 1/3 cups cocoa powder
1 tsp salt

Directions

1. Preheat oven to 325°F. Grease a 9"x13" pan.
2. In a 2 qt. high-sided mixing bowl and using an electric mixer, beat together the melted butter, oil, and sugar for 3 minutes at medium-high speed. Reduce speed to medium and beat in eggs and vanilla.
3. In another large mixing bowl, whisk together the dry ingredients (flour, cocoa powder, and salt.)
4. Pour the dry ingredients into the wet ingredients, stirring mixture by hand with a wooden spoon, until ingredients are thoroughly combined. (Brownie batter will be very thick.) Spread batter into greased 9"x13" pan.
5. Bake for 20-25 minutes at 325°F or until an inserted fork comes out mostly clean. Don't overbake. (These brownies are best when removed slightly gooey inside.)
6. Cut and serve when cool. *Enjoy!* W

Note: Store any remaining brownies in a covered container or zip plastic bag to keep them fresh.

Frosted Buttermilk Brownies

(A yummy, light brownie like a Texas sheet cake. Serves 24+)

Buttermilk Brownies

1 cup water
½ cup butter
½ cup vegetable oil
2 cups sugar
2 cups flour
3 Tbl cocoa powder
2 eggs
1 tsp baking soda
½ cup buttermilk (or use buttermilk substitute: ½ cup plain Greek yogurt, or ½ cup whole milk + 1½ tsp vinegar)

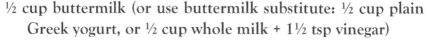

Directions

1. Preheat oven to 400°F. Grease two 9"x13" pans or grease one low-sided jelly roll pan approximately 13"x18"x1".
2. In a small saucepan, combine water, butter, and vegetable oil. Place pan over medium heat on stove. Bring mixture to a boil, then remove from heat. (Alternatively, heating ingredients in a glass dish in microwave oven is great, too.)
3. In a 2 qt. high-sided mixing bowl, whisk together sugar, flour, and cocoa powder. Over this mixture, pour the hot saucepan ingredients. Use an electric mixer at medium-speed to beat the combination until creamy. Reduce speed to low and beat in remaining ingredients (eggs, baking soda, and buttermilk) until well mixed. Pour into greased pan(s).
4. Bake at 400°F for 18 minutes. (While brownies are baking, prepare frosting.) Remove brownies from oven when edges are lightly brown. Let them cool for 10 minutes.
5. While still slightly warm, frost with **Buttermilk Brownie Frosting.** *Mmmm good!* E

Buttermilk Brownie Frosting

½ cup butter

3 Tbl cocoa powder

1/3 cup buttermilk (or use buttermilk substitute: 1/3 cup plain Greek yogurt, or 1/3 cup milk + 1 tsp vinegar)

3¾ cups powdered sugar, sifted

½ tsp vanilla

Directions

1. In a 2 or 3 qt. heavy-bottom saucepan, combine butter, cocoa powder, and buttermilk (or its substitute.) Place pan over medium heat on stove. Stir mixture constantly with a wire whisk—scraping the bottom of the pan so it doesn't burn—until mixture boils, then remove from heat.
2. Into this pan, whisk in sifted powdered sugar and vanilla.
3. Spoon onto warm (not hot) brownies and smooth over top.

Note: Any extra brownie frosting freezes well in a sealed container or zip plastic freezer bag.

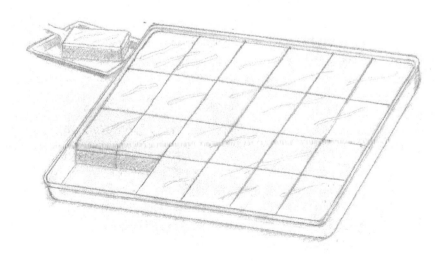

Rice Crispy Treats

(This traditional treat can be cut or shaped into castles or anything you want. *Be creative! Have fun!* Serves 18+)

7 cups dry crispy cereal*
6 Tbl butter
1 pkg (16 oz.) marshmallows**

Directions

1. Grease a 9" x 13" pan *and* a large 12 qt. mixing bowl.
2. Measure 7 cups dry cereal into large, greased mixing bowl.
3. Melt butter with marshmallows in one of these two ways:
   A. **On the stove**—combine both ingredients in a 2 qt. heavy-bottom saucepan over low heat and stir until melted. OR
   B. **In the microwave**—combine both ingredients in a 2 qt. microwave-safe bowl and cook for 1 minute. Stir down mixture with silicone spatula. Reheat and stir in 15 second intervals until marshmallows fully melt.
4. Pour marshmallow mixture over dry cereal and stir together.
5. Pour cereal mixture into greased 9"x13" pan and gently press into place with greased fingers or an inverted butter wrapper.
6. Cool completely—about 30 minutes—and cut into 2" squares or into desired shapes. *So yummy!*

Note: For a smaller batch, use an 8" or 9" square pan, 4 Tbl butter, one 10 oz. bag marshmallows**, and 4 2/3 cups dry crispy cereal. Follow directions above. *Enjoy!* S

*Rice Crispies are the traditional choice of cereal, but any packaged, dry breakfast cereal will work. *Have fun!*
**Both mini or large marshmallows work with this recipe.

Lemon Bars

(So pretty *and* delicious! Makes 24 wonderful, 2" squares.)

<u>Pastry Crust</u>
1 cup butter, softened
½ cup powdered sugar
2 cups flour

<u>Lemon Filling</u>
4 eggs
1½ cups sugar
¼ cup flour
5 Tbl lemon juice (juice of 2 lemons)

<u>Top Sprinkle</u>: ½ cup powdered sugar, sifted

Directions
<u>Pastry Crust</u>:
1. Preheat oven to 350°F. Set out a 9"x13" ungreased pan.
2. In a 2 qt. high-sided mixing bowl, use an electric mixer at medium-high speed to cream the softened butter and powdered sugar for 1 minute. Beat in the flour. Press this dough evenly into the bottom of the 9"x13" ungreased pan.
3. Bake at 350°F, 15 minutes or until crust is lightly browned. Remove crust from oven. Cool slightly. (Keep oven hot.)

<u>Lemon Filling</u>:
1. In an 8 cup batter bowl, whisk together eggs, sugar, flour and lemon juice. Pour mixture onto warm crust in 9"x13" pan.
2. Place in oven and bake at 350°F for 15-20 minutes (or until filling no longer jiggles.) Cool completely.

<u>Top Sprinkle</u>: Sift powdered sugar over top of cooled lemon filling. Cut into 2" squares. *Serve and enjoy!* N

Oatmeal-Berry Bars

(These wonderful little bars are "berry" delicious! Serves 24.)

Crust
1½ cups rolled oats (not quick oats)
1½ cups flour
1 cup brown sugar
½ tsp baking soda
¾ cup butter, melted
Berry Filling
½ cup sugar
2 Tbl cornstarch
2 Tbl lemon juice
2 cups mixed berries (may use frozen)

Directions
Crust and Crumb Topping:
1. In a 2 qt. high-sided mixing bowl, whisk flour, oats, brown sugar, and baking soda together. Pour melted butter over dry ingredients and stir with spoon until combined.
2. Reserve 2 cups of this oat mixture for Crumb Topping.
3. Press remaining oat mixture into a greased 9"x13" pan.
Berry filling:
1. In 2-3 qt. heavy-bottom pot, mix all Berry Filling ingredients.
2. Place pot over medium heat on stove. While stirring constantly with silicone spatula, bring mixture to a boil. Cook for 2 minutes. Remove Berry Filling from heat.
Completion:
1. Preheat oven to 375°F. Carefully pour the Berry Filling over the oat Crust in the pan. Sprinkle reserved oat Crumb Topping evenly over Berry Filling.
2. Bake for 25 minutes. Cool before cutting into 2" bars. *Great!*

My Own Brownie Recipes:

Recipe:

Recipe:

Recipe:

"It was a dark and stormy knight," typed Tim Wright.

"Tim, you misspelled the word *knight*," said Kimberly, glancing over his shoulder. "It's supposed to be spelled *night*."

"No, this knight's kind of grumpy," said Tim. "He goes around bopping people on the head all the time."

"Now why would a knight do that?" asked Kimberly.

"Oh, he doesn't do it at night, only during the day."

"Great, so now we've got a dark and stormy knight, during the day, because it's not night," said Kimberly. "Tim, where do you come up with all these ideas?"

"I didn't come up with it," said Tim. "He's standing right behind you."

Kimberly turned and shrieked, "Jonathan Wright, you take off that costume armor right now!"

"I can't," chuckled Jonathan, "Mom put me on guard duty to keep you two out of the kitchen while she puts the surprise in the Surprise Chocolate Cupcakes."

—CAKES, CUPCAKES, & SWEET BREADS —

"The Great Cupcake Adventure"

- o Birthday Cake-in-a-Cup
- o Carrot Cake with Cream Cheese Frosting
- o Surprise Chocolate Cupcakes
- o Best Banana Bread
- o Pumpkin Bread
- o Gingerbread
- o Blueberry Muffins
- o Apple Spice Muffins

World-renowned poet, artist, and all-around good guy, Timothy Wright, esquire, has just decorated his first large piece of Carrot Cake. He has carefully drawn on, with frosting, orange carrot-people with green eyes, mouths, and various hats—cowboy, crowns, helmets, funny hair—onto a white background. Look at that INCREDIBLE masterpiece—oops, he just ate it!

Birthday Cake-in-a-Cup

(A delightful little cake with sprinkles! Make it quickly in the microwave, add whipped cream, a colorful candle, and give it to your favorite person on their birthday! So fun! Makes one single-serve, delicious mini cake in a ceramic mug or cup.)

4 Tbl flour
1½ Tbl sugar
½ tsp baking powder
4 Tbl milk
1½ Tbl melted butter
¼ tsp vanilla
1½ tsp candy sprinkles

Optional toppings:
Whipped Cream, Frosting, or a scoop of Vanilla Ice Cream
Birthday Candle

Directions
1. Using a microwave-safe mug or cup, add the flour, sugar, and baking powder. Stir together with a fork.
2. Add remaining ingredients (milk, melted butter, vanilla, candy sprinkles) and stir with fork until thoroughly moistened.
3. Cook in microwave 50 seconds or until cake is set. (Microwave ovens vary in wattage and cooking times.)
4. Cool in mug. Add optional toppings. Serve! So easy! So fun! They'll love it!

Note: A common, low calorie substitution for butter is applesauce. If you use applesauce in this recipe, also add a slight sprinkle of salt.

This recipe also makes a darling packaged birthday "Gift in a Mug." You'll want to:

- Get a cute mug, a clear gift bag, a colorful birthday candle, and some pretty curling ribbon. Copy the "Birthday Cake just for YOU!" card below.
- Bag-up just the recipe's dry ingredients (including the candy sprinkles) in the clear gift bag. Close bag with a twist tie.
- Neatly cut out the copied card. Punch a hole in its top left corner. Tape a colorful birthday candle onto card.
- Run curling ribbon through the card's hole and tie card to dry ingredient's bag. Curl ends of ribbon.
- Place bag in mug. Voila! Cute birthday present!

A BIRTHDAY CAKE just for YOU!

Instructions:
1. Wash and dry mug before use.
2. Pour bag's contents into mug. Add: 4 Tbl milk, 1½ Tbl melted butter & ¼ tsp vanilla. Stir with fork.
3. Microwave 50 sec. or until cake's surface is set. Cool. (Or bake in oven at 350°F, 12-14 min. or until cake is set.)
4. Add a topping if you want (like whipped cream). Insert birthday candle, light it, make a wish, and blow it out! Know that you are loved and you are a special person in this world!
5. Enjoy every bite of your mini cake and have a very Happy Birthday!

Carrot Cake with Cream Cheese Frosting

(This is Grandma Julie's luscious carrot cake. It has a *secret* moist ingredient! It's so delicious! The batch fills three 9" round cake pans or one 9"x13" pan or one 12-cup Bundt cake pan or 36 muffin cups. Wonderful! Serves 24-36)

<u>Carrot Cake</u>
2 cups flour, sifted
2 tsp baking powder
½ tsp baking soda
1 tsp salt
2 tsp cinnamon
1 cup vegetable oil
2 cups carrot chunks
4 eggs

1 cup canned pineapple, drained (use any form of canned pineapple – it will be blended, so it doesn't matter if it's originally in rings, chunks or crushed form)
1½ cups sugar
(Optional) 1 cup chopped walnuts or pecans

Directions
1. In an 8-cup batter bowl, whisk together the sifted flour, baking powder, baking soda, salt, and cinnamon. Set aside.
2. In an electric blender, mix together the remaining ingredients, as follows:
   A. Blend vegetable oil and carrot chunks on medium speed until carrots are finely shredded.
   B. Add eggs and pineapple (*secret moist ingredient.*) Blend together on low speed until thoroughly mixed.

C. Add sugar and optional chopped nuts and blend together briefly on low speed.

3. Preheat oven to 350°F. Grease and flour baking pans of your choice (Three 9" cake pans or 9"x 13" pan or 12-cup Bundt cake pan or 36 muffin cups lined with paper cupcake liners.)

4. Pour blended mixture into the 8-cup batter bowl holding the dry ingredients. Stir gently with large spoon just until combined. Pour into greased and floured baking pans.

5. Bake until an inserted toothpick comes out clean. (Cooking time: 12-cup Bundt pan = about 60 minutes, Three 9" cake pans = 30-40 minutes, 36 Cupcakes = 18-24 minutes.)

<u>Cream Cheese Frosting</u> (double this to frost a 3 layer cake)
½ cup butter, softened
8 oz. pkg. cream cheese, softened to room temperature
1 tsp vanilla
¼ tsp lemon juice
pinch salt
4 cups powdered confectioner's sugar, sifted
(Optional) 1 Tbl milk (to make a thinner frosting, if desired)

Directions
1. In a large mixing bowl, use an electric mixer at medium-high speed to cream together the softened butter and cream cheese for 1 minute. At low speed, beat in vanilla, lemon juice, and salt.

2. Slowly add sifted powdered sugar, beating on low, until well combined. Thin with milk, if desired. ＭＭ

3. Frost cooled **Carrot Cake**. *Enjoy!*
(If frosting a 3-layer carrot cake, use ¾ to 1 cup frosting in between layers and frost top and sides as well.)

Note: Freeze extra frosting in a zip freezer bag up to 3 months.

Surprise Chocolate Cupcakes

(Ready to surprise your family? Make up these delicious cupcakes and use the Chocolate or Vanilla Frosting as a topping—or hide it secretly inside each one. They're fabulous! Makes 24 chocolate cupcakes)

<u>Chocolate Cupcakes</u>

1½ cups flour
2/3 cup cocoa powder*
1½ cups sugar
2 Tbl brown sugar
1½ tsp baking soda
¾ tsp salt
1½ cups milk
2 eggs
2 tsp white vinegar
½ cup vegetable oil
1 tsp vanilla

Directions

1. Preheat oven to 325°F. Line muffin tins with 24 paper cupcake liners.
2. In an 8-cup batter bowl, whisk together the flour, cocoa powder, sugar, brown sugar, baking soda, and salt.
3. In a 4-cup bowl, stir together the milk, eggs, vinegar, oil, and vanilla with a fork.
4. Pour the liquid mixture over the dry ingredients in the batter bowl. Whisk together until batter is smooth.
5. Fill each cupcake liner 2/3 full with batter.
6. Bake at 325°F for 18-20 minutes or until an inserted toothpick comes out clean. Cool cupcakes on wire rack.

*Note: Hershey's Cocoa 100% Cacao Natural Unsweetened

Chocolate Frosting
*1 cup butter, softened
3½ cups powdered sugar, sifted
½ cup cocoa powder, sifted
3 Tbl milk or **heavy whipping cream
2 tsp vanilla

Vanilla Frosting
*1 cup butter, softened
4 cups powdered sugar, sifted
1/8 tsp salt
6 Tbl milk or **heavy whipping cream
2 tsp vanilla

Directions to make either Chocolate or Vanilla frosting:
1. Make frosting: Using a 2 qt. high-sided mixing bowl and an electric mixer, cream the softened butter for 30 seconds. Blend in the dry ingredients for 2-3 minutes, until mixture is moist and clings together. Beat in milk or cream and vanilla.
2. Fill cupcakes: To squirt the Frosting inside like a filling, use a medium size decorator's piping tip on a pastry bag. Fill bag with Frosting. Insert tip into the top center of a cupcake and squirt in a little frosting. Repeat until all cupcakes are filled. Frost over tops of cupcakes. *Serve and enjoy!*

*Note: For a less buttery taste in either of these recipes, use ½ cup butter plus ½ cup vegetable shortening.

**Note: If a light, airy texture is desired for your frosting, use heavy whipping cream instead of milk. Add cream to mixture and beat 4-5 minutes until fluffy, then stir in vanilla. *Great!*

Best Banana Bread

(So yummy! Our favorite use of overripe bananas. Makes 1 moist loaf, cut into 12, 3/4" thick slices, or 12 muffins.)

1¾ cups flour, sifted
2 tsp baking powder
¼ tsp baking soda
¼ tsp salt
½ cup butter, softened
2 Tbl vegetable oil
2/3 cup sugar
2 eggs, well beaten
1 cup mashed, overripe bananas (about 2-3 bananas)

Directions
1. Preheat oven to 350°F. Grease a 9" loaf pan.
2. In a 4 cup bowl, whisk together the **dry ingredients** (sifted flour, baking powder, baking soda, salt.)
3. In a 2 qt. high-sided mixing bowl, use an electric mixer to cream together the softened butter, oil, and sugar for 2 minutes at medium-high speed until mixture is fluffy. Add in eggs and beat another minute at medium speed.
4. Add the dry ingredients into the creamed sugar mixture. Blend together on medium speed until combined. Add mashed bananas and blend on low speed until evenly mixed. Pour batter into greased loaf pan.
5. Bake at 350°F for 45 minutes or until loaf top is lightly browned and an inserted toothpick comes out clean.
6. Cool in the pan. Slice and serve.

Author Greg's hint: For a stronger, yummy flavor, eat all the crust off your slice first, then squish the rest of the slice into a ball and enjoy!

Pumpkin Bread

(Super moist and delicious! Makes 2 yummy loaves
or 24 muffins)

2 cups canned pumpkin (or one 15 oz. can)
1 cup brown sugar (or substitute with 1 cup white sugar plus
   1 Tbl molasses)
1 cup sugar
½ cup vegetable oil
½ tsp vanilla
2½ cups flour, sifted
2 tsp baking soda
½ tsp salt
1 tsp cinnamon
½ tsp cloves

Directions

1. Preheat oven to 350°F. Grease two 9" loaf pans.
2. In an 8-cup batter bowl, use an electric mixer at medium speed to blend together the pumpkin, brown sugar (or its substitute), sugar, and vegetable oil. Gently mix in vanilla.
3. In a 4-cup bowl, whisk together the flour, baking soda, salt, cinnamon, and cloves.
4. Add the dry ingredients to the wet ingredients and beat together on low speed until fully combined. Batter will be thick. Pour into greased loaf pans.
5. Bake at 350°F for 50 minutes or until an inserted knife comes out clean.
6. Let cool completely in pans. Slice and serve. *Wonderful!*

Note: This bread stores well when wrapped in aluminum foil and kept at room temperature for several days. Freezes well, too.

Gingerbread

(A tasty delight on a cold winter day! Makes 24 muffins or one 9"x13" unfrosted pan of delicious gingerbread.)

½ cup butter, melted
¼ cup vegetable oil
1 cup molasses
1 cup water
½ cup sugar
2 eggs
3 1/3 cups flour, sifted
1½ tsp baking soda
1½ tsp ginger
1½ tsp cinnamon
1 tsp salt

Directions

1. Preheat oven to 325°F. Grease a 9"x13" pan.
2. In an 8-cup batter bowl, use an electric mixer at medium speed to beat together the butter, oil, molasses, water, sugar, and eggs until blended.
3. In another mixing bowl, whisk together the sifted flour, baking soda, ginger, cinnamon, and salt. Pour the dry ingredients into the batter bowl. Beat together on medium speed until thoroughly combined, occasionally scraping bowl. Pour batter into greased pan.
4. Bake at 325°F for 25-30 minutes or until an inserted toothpick comes out clean.
5. Serve with or without whipped cream. *Delicious!*

Note: For Gingerbread Muffins, heat oven to 350°F. Grease 24 muffin tins or apply cupcake liners. Fill muffin tins 2/3 full. Bake 12-16 min. or until an inserted toothpick comes out clean.

Blueberry Muffins

(Need a big bite of blueberry? Try these fabulous muffins!
Makes 12 tasty muffins)

½ cup butter, softened
2/3 cup sugar
½ cup milk
2 eggs
1 tsp vanilla
2 cups flour
½ tsp salt
2 tsp baking powder
1 tsp organic lemon zest
2 cups blueberries

Directions

1. Preheat oven to 375°F. Grease 12 muffin cups or line with cupcake liners.
2. In an 8-cup batter bowl, cream the softened butter and sugar with an electric mixer on medium-high speed. Beat in the milk, eggs, and vanilla briefly at medium speed.
3. In a 4-cup bowl, whisk together the flour, salt, baking powder, and lemon zest. Pour the dry ingredients into the wet ingredients.
4. Mix together at medium speed until batter is thoroughly moistened. Gently fold in the blueberries.
5. Fill muffin cups evenly with batter. (A greased ice cream scoop or cookie scoop works well for this.)
6. Bake at 375°F for 16-18 minutes or until golden brown on top. Cool on wire rack. *Enjoy!* 　B

Apple Spice Muffins

(Flavorful & moist! A fresh taste of Fall! Makes 24 muffins)

3 cups flour
1¼ cups sugar
2 tsp baking soda
¾ tsp salt
1½ tsp ground cinnamon
¼ tsp ground cloves, heaping
¼ tsp ground nutmeg, heaping
1 cup milk or water
2 eggs
1 cup applesauce
½ cup melted butter or vegetable oil
1½ tsp vanilla
2 apples*, grated or diced
(Optional) ¾ cup chopped walnuts, ¾ cup raisins

Directions

1. Preheat oven to 350°F. Grease 24 muffin tins with baking spray or line with cupcake liners.
2. In an 8-cup batter bowl, whisk together the dry ingredients (flour, sugar, baking soda, salt, cinnamon, cloves, nutmeg.)
3. In a 4-cup liquid measuring cup, mix together the wet ingredients with a fork (milk, eggs, applesauce, melted butter and vanilla.) Pour wet ingredients into dry ingredients in batter bowl. Add diced apples and desired optional ingredients. Mix with a large spoon, just until the batter is moistened. Spoon batter evenly into muffin tins.
4. Bake at 350°F for 20-24 minutes or until an inserted toothpick comes out clean. Cool on wire rack. *Delicious!*

*Note: Kids love grated apples. Adults often prefer diced apples.

My Own Cake Recipes:

Recipes:

_____

_____

_____

_____

_____

_____

_____

_____

_____

_____

_____

_____

_____

_____

_____

_____

_____

_____

_____

_____

_____

_____

_____

_____

_____

The five Wright cousins had been working in their grandparents' orchard all morning.

"I can't wait to get some of that ice cream Grandma promised us," said 17-year-old Robert Wright as they headed back to the ranch house.

"Is it Grandma's homemade ice cream or the stuff from the store?" said Tim.

"Grandma's," Robert replied.

"Awesome," said Tim, "dibbs on the biggest bowl!"

"Sorry, Tim," said Lindy, "Grandma always reserves that one for Grandpa."

"I'll wash out the dog's water bowl, then," said Tim.

— ICE CREAM TREATS —

"Secret Agents *Definitely* Like Ice Cream!"

- o   Tips for Making Ice Cream
- o   Classic Vanilla Ice Cream
- o   Light Homemade Ice Cream
- o   Ultra-Creamy Ice Cream
- o   Mint Chocolate Chip Ice Cream
- o   Chocolate Chip Ice Cream
- o   Chocolate Ice Cream
- o   Candy Bar Crunch/Cookie Crumble Ice Cream
- o   Strawberry Ice Cream
- o   Orange Creamsicle
- o   Raspberry Sherbet
- o   Orange Sherbet
- o   Berry Good Sauce
- o   Chocolate Syrup
- o   Mint Grasshopper Pie

"Yodel-Lay-Hee-Hoo"

Let your spoon do the skiing! ENJOY the ADVENTURE!

61

Tips for Making Ice Cream

1. Make sure all ice cream equipment is thoroughly clean.
2. A hint when making ice cream: whisk liquid ingredients together inside a tall beverage pitcher, lid, and refrigerate. When ready, pour contents easily into the ice cream maker.
3. If your family likes frequent batches of homemade ice cream, it's economical to use a 1.5 qt. or 2 qt. double-insulated freezer bowl ice cream maker, like Cuisinart's. These makers don't require ice or rock salt. Instead, they use an insulated bowl that's kept in your freezer. Just pull out the bowl whenever you're ready to make up a quick 20 minute batch of delicious ice cream.
4. For large party events with 16 or more people, you can use an old fashioned ice/salt ice cream maker. These churn out ice cream in about 30 minutes. Both the hand crank and electric models work great. (Do keep extra crushed ice and rock salt handy, though. You don't want to accidentally run out in the middle of your freezing/churning process.)

Ice & Salt Needed for Old Fashioned Ice Cream Makers:

Ice Cream Maker Size	No. of People Served	Pounds of Crushed Ice	Rock Salt
6 qt.	24	14-21	3-5 cups
4 qt.	16	10-16	2-3 cups

Classic Vanilla Ice Cream

(This is Grandma Dorothy Smith's famous homemade ice cream enjoyed by generations. Using 2% milk makes the ice cream slightly sweeter. *It's smooth and wonderful!*)

1.5 qt. Ice Cream Maker

1 egg
½ cup sugar
1 Tbl vanilla*
1/8 tsp salt, heaping
1½ cups half & half
2 cups milk (2% or whole)

2 qt. Ice Cream Maker

2 eggs
2/3 cup sugar
1½ Tbl vanilla*
¼ tsp salt, scant
2 cups half & half
2 2/3 cups milk (2% or whole)

4 qt. Ice Cream Maker

3 eggs
1¼ cups sugar
3 Tbl vanilla*
½ tsp salt, scant
1 qt. half & half
5 cups milk (2% or whole)

Directions: Whisk ingredients together in a tall beverage pitcher or bowl with a spout. Follow your ice cream maker's instructions for the churning process, usually taking 20-30 minutes. Enjoy!

*Note: Molina Mexican Vanilla Blend is our preferred vanilla, with its rich flavor and extremely low alcohol content.

Light Homemade Ice Cream

(Author Greg's favorite! Cool, thirst quenching, low in calories, and inexpensive to make. *It's simply delicious!*)

<u>1.5 qt. Ice Cream Maker</u>
1 egg
½ cup sugar, heaping
2 Tbl powdered milk
2¼ tsp vanilla*
1/8 tsp salt
3 cups 2% milk

<u>2 qt. Ice Cream Maker</u> ☺
1 egg
3/4 cup sugar
3 Tbl powdered milk
1 Tbl vanilla*
1/8 tsp salt, heaping
4½ cups 2% milk

<u>4 qt. Ice Cream Maker</u>
3 eggs
1½ cups sugar, heaping
5 Tbl powdered milk
2 Tbl vanilla*
¼ tsp salt
9 cups 2% milk

Directions: Whisk ingredients together in a tall beverage pitcher or bowl with a spout. Follow your ice cream maker's instructions for the churning process, usually taking 20-30 minutes. Enjoy!

***Molina Mexican Vanilla Blend** is our preferred vanilla.

Ultra-Creamy Ice Cream

(Known in our family as Ken's "High Octane" Ice Cream.
This one is super yummy!)

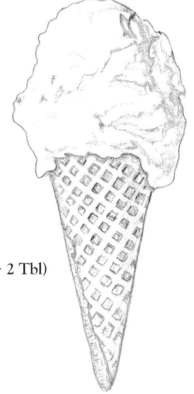

1.5 qt. Ice Cream Maker
¾ cup heavy whipping cream
4 Tbl sugar, heaping
1½ tsp vanilla*
½ cup evaporated milk
½ scant cup swtnd. cond. milk
2 cups whole milk

2 qt. Ice Cream Maker
1 cup heavy whipping cream
6 Tbl sugar, heaping
2 tsp vanilla*
½ can evaporated milk, (2/3 cup)
½ can swtnd. cond. milk, (½ cup + 2 Tbl)
3 cups whole milk

4 qt. Ice Cream Maker
1 pint heavy whipping cream
¾ cup sugar, heaping
4 tsp vanilla*
1 can evaporated milk, 12 oz. (1 1/3 cups)
1 can sweetened condensed milk, 14 oz. (1¼ cups)
6 cups whole milk

Directions: Whisk ingredients together in a tall beverage pitcher or bowl with a spout. Follow your ice cream maker's instructions for the churning process, usually taking 20-30 minutes. Enjoy!

*****Note: Molina Mexican Vanilla Blend** is our preferred vanilla.

Fun Ice Cream Flavors

(Many flavors of ice cream start with a vanilla ice cream base and simply, but deliciously, build upon it. Notice how the next 6 recipes delightfully change-up a 1.5 qt. batch of Vanilla Ice Cream with just a few additions. Find your favorite flavor!)

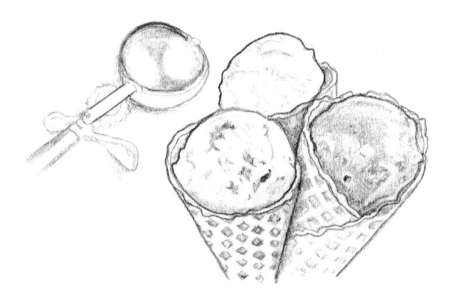

Mint Chocolate Chip

1.5 qt. Vanilla Ice Cream ingredients, plus...
5 drops of green food coloring
3-4 drops of peppermint oil*
<u>Chocolate Drizzle</u>
1/3 cup semisweet chocolate chips
2 tsp vegetable oil

Directions

1. In a large beverage pitcher or bowl with a spout, whisk together a 1.5 qt. batch of vanilla ice cream plus green food coloring and peppermint oil.
2. Pour mixture into ice cream maker's spinning freezer bowl.
3. After 15 minutes, prepare the **Chocolate Drizzle**: In a small microwaveable cup, add the chocolate chips and vegetable oil. Microwave for 30 seconds. Stir and reheat briefly, as needed, until chocolate is smooth and runny.
4. Pour melted chocolate slowly into churning ice cream as a thin, steady drizzle. (The chocolate will freeze and break into tiny bits in the swirling cream.)
5. Let the ice cream maker continue churning until ice cream is fluffy, thick, and ready to enjoy!   J

*Note: LorAnn Oils Super-Strength Peppermint Oil is our favorite food grade peppermint oil often used in candy making. It does *not* taste like toothpaste. Yay!

Chocolate Chip Ice Cream

1.5 qt. Vanilla Ice Cream ingredients, plus...
<u>Chocolate Drizzle</u>
1/3 cup semisweet chocolate chips
2 tsp vegetable oil

Directions
1. Whisk together a 1.5 qt. batch of vanilla ice cream. Start it going in your ice cream maker.
2. After 15 minutes of churning, prepare the **Chocolate Drizzle**: In a small microwaveable cup, add the chocolate chips and vegetable oil. Microwave for 30 seconds. Stir and reheat briefly, as needed, until chocolate is smooth and runny.
3. Pour melted chocolate slowly into churning ice cream as a thin, steady drizzle. (The chocolate will freeze and break into tiny bits in the swirling cream.)
4. Let the ice cream maker continue churning until ice cream is fluffy, thick, and ready to enjoy. *Wonderful!*

Chocolate Ice Cream

1.5 qt. Vanilla Ice Cream ingredients, plus...
¼ cup Chocolate Syrup
(or substitute: 4 Tbl cocoa powder + ¼ cup more white sugar)

Directions: Whisk together 1.5 qt. vanilla ice cream ingredients with chocolate ingredients in a large pitcher or bowl with a spout. Pour mixture into ice cream maker's spinning bowl. Churn/freeze 20 minutes or until ice cream is *frosty and smooth!*

Candy Bar Crunch or Cookie Crumble Ice Cream

1.5 qt. Vanilla Ice Cream, plus...
5 oz. (½ cup) favorite candy bar bits (i.e. Butterfingers, Snickers, Reese's Peanut Butter Cups,...) P
or
½ cup favorite cookie crumbles (i.e. Oreo's, Coconut Dreams, Grasshopper/Thin Mints, Mother's Circus...)

Directions: Make up a 1.5 qt. batch of vanilla ice cream. During the last 2 minutes of churning/freezing, add ½ cup of your favorite candy bar pieces or ½ cup favorite cookie crumbles.

Hint- Garnish each Cookie Crumble ice cream serving with a whole cookie on top. *So pretty and soooo yummy!*

Strawberry Ice Cream

1.5 qt. Vanilla Ice Cream ingredients, plus...
1½ cups strawberries, pureed
¼ cup sugar
1 tsp lemon juice
(Optional) sliced fresh strawberries

Directions: In a blender, puree 1½ cups strawberries. On low speed, mix in vanilla ice cream ingredients, ¼ cup more sugar, and lemon juice. Pour mixture into ice cream maker's spinning bowl. Churn/freeze 20 minutes or until ice cream is smooth and thick. Serve ice cream with fresh strawberry slices on the side as a lovely garnish. *Wonderful!*

Orange Creamsicle

1.5 qt. Vanilla Ice Cream ingredients, plus...
1 cup orange juice
½ cup sugar, heaping
Orange Flavoring (either: 1 Tbl orange zest or 4 drops pure orange oil or 1 tsp orange extract)

Directions: In a large bowl with a spout, whisk together vanilla ice cream ingredients, orange juice, additional sugar, and your choice of orange flavoring. Pour mix into ice cream maker's spinning bowl. Churn/freeze 20 minutes or until ice cream is smooth & creamy. Serve soft or freeze in popsicle molds. *Enjoy!*

Raspberry Sherbet

(Notice how sherbets use about twice as much whole fruit as they do milk. They're so smooth and *deliciously refreshing!*)

3 cups raspberries (fresh or frozen)
1½ cups whole milk
¾ cup sugar, heaping
1¼ tsp lemon juice

Directions: Puree all ingredients in a blender. Remove raspberry seeds by pouring the puree through a fine sieve into a large bowl. (Use a spatula to work it through the sieve.) Discard the seeds. Pour mixture into the ice cream maker's spinning bowl. Churn/freeze 20 minutes. Serve it soft or place in freezer to harden longer. *Excellent!*

Orange Sherbet

3 cups freshly squeezed orange juice
Orange Flavoring (either 2 Tbl finely grated orange zest or 4 drops pure orange oil or 1 tsp orange extract)
1½ Tbl lemon juice
1½ tsp vanilla
2/3 cup sugar
¼ tsp salt
2¼ cups whole milk

Directions: Whisk all ingredients together thoroughly in a large pitcher or a bowl with a spout. Pour into ice cream maker's spinning bowl. Churn/freeze 20 minutes. Serve it soft or harden 1 hour longer in a freezer. *It's amazing!*

Berry Good Sauce

(Serve this delicious berry sauce swirled into a bowl of Vanilla Ice Cream! It's also a lovely topping for Cheese Cake, French Toast, Pancakes, or Waffles. Makes 1¼ cups berry sauce.)

2 cups berries*
2 Tbl lemon juice (or less)
½ cup sugar
1 Tbl cornstarch
Optional garnish:
¼ cup whole berries*

Directions
1. In blender, puree together 2 cups berries and lemon juice.
2. In a small, heavy bottom saucepan, stir together sugar, cornstarch, and berry-lemon puree with a silicone spatula. Cook over medium heat, stirring occasionally—scraping bottom of pan—until mixture boils. Reduce temperature to low and continue cooking and stirring for one more minute.
3. Remove from heat. Pour berry sauce into a pretty serving dish.
4. Serve hot or cold (possibly with a few whole berries as an optional topping). *So good!*
5. Store any extra sauce in a lidded mason jar or other covered container in the refrigerator or freezer.

*Note: Use either fresh or frozen whole berries. (Try mixed berries, strawberries, blueberries, blackberries...they are all *wonderful* in this recipe!) F

Chocolate Syrup

(Easy to make and soooo good! Simple ingredients! No corn syrup. No chemical taste. Just total deliciousness! Far better than commercial brands! Makes 1½ cups chocolate syrup.)

1 cup sugar
½ cup cocoa powder*
½ cup milk
1 Tbl butter
2 tsp Mexican vanilla**

Directions

1. In a small, heavy bottom saucepan, whisk together sugar and cocoa powder. Whisk in milk, making a runny paste. Add butter.
2. Place saucepan with chocolate mixture over medium heat on stove. Stir with silicone spatula until butter melts and mixture begins to boil. Reduce heat to medium-low and simmer, stirring constantly for 1 minute. (By stirring constantly and scraping the bottom of the pan, you will keep the syrup from burning.)
3. Remove from heat. Stir in vanilla. Pour syrup into glass mason jar or a pretty serving dish. Syrup will naturally thicken as it cools.
4. Drizzle syrup over ice cream, as desired. *Enjoy every spoonful!*

Note: If syrup thickens too much for your use, briefly microwave in a glass container in 20 second intervals, stirring between heating times. Refrigerate any extra syrup in lidded container. Use within 2 weeks.

* We use **Hershey's Cocoa 100% Cacao Natural Unsweetened**
****Molina Mexican Vanilla Blend** is our preferred vanilla.

Mint Grasshopper Pie ☺

("For my birthday, please!" says Tim Wright. "Is it really made with grasshoppers?" A birthday party favorite! Makes 1, 9" pie.)

28 Oreo cookies, ground (or about 2¼ cups)
1/3 cup butter, melted
1.5 qt. Mint Chocolate Chip Ice Cream

Directions

1. Make the **Oreo Cookie Crust**: In blender or food processer at low speed, grind 28 Oreo cookies into 1/8" crumb size. (Set aside ¼ cup for optional garnish topping.) Melt butter in a large glass bowl in microwave for about 25 seconds. Mix in 2 cups cookie crumbs. Press this mixture evenly into the bottom and sides of a 9" pie pan.
2. Soften mint chocolate chip ice cream slightly. Spread into cookie crust using silicone spatula to smooth top.
3. Cover whole pie with plastic wrap and freeze at least 1 hour.
4. Prior to serving, defrost pie for 10 minutes. Remove plastic from top. Sprinkle with optional cookie crumb garnish. Cut and serve. *Totally Delicious for summer parties and all year long!*

My Own Ice Cream Recipes:

Recipe:

Recipe:

Recipe:

"Okay," said Kimberly Wright, "I think we've got everything ready for our Wright family movie night...the movie, the popcorn, the treats. We've got the ingredients to make up the hot chocolate during the intermission. Our cousins should be here in about five minutes."

"Kimberly," said her younger brother, Tim, "there's something I don't understand about time."

"What's that?" said Kimberly.

"Well, for one thing, it's not all the same," Tim replied. "Have you ever noticed how it sneaks around and speeds up and slows down?"

"Tim, time is time. It always stays the same."

"Then why, when you cook something in the toaster, it takes forever. The toaster just keeps cooking and cooking as long as you watch it. And the microwave...I put something in it for 4 minutes and while it's counting down, it must sneak a bunch of extra numbers in there and it takes at least 10 minutes."

"We could check it with your watch," Kimberly suggested.

"I don't think that would help," said Tim. "When you suspect something, all the clocks start covering for each other and act like they're all keeping the same time."

"Tim, did you know that in the old days they had a way to totally stop time?"

"Really?" said Tim.

"Yes," Kimberly said, "they just didn't wind up their clocks."

"Arrgh, *sisters*," said Tim.

— REFRESHINGLY FUN DRINKS —

"Ladies and gentlemen, grab your straws!"

- o Strawberry Thing
- o Ice Cold Lemonade
- o Homemade Hot Chocolate
- o Hot Apple Cider
- o Raspberry Party Fizz

Strawberry Thing

(A smooth and delicious strawberry smoothie! Growing up in the desert, author Greg's family made this as a great thirst quenching, sweet drink. Serves 4–Tim Wright says it serves 1)

2 cups milk
2 cups frozen strawberries
¼ cup sugar (or more to taste)

Directions
1. Add all ingredients into blender pitcher. Add more sugar to taste, if desired.
2. Blend on high speed until strawberries are fully pulverized and milk is lusciously thick and a pretty pink. Turn off blender before mixture gets foamy.
3. Pour into glasses. Add straws. *Enjoy!*

G

Ice Cold Lemonade

(Pretty and thirst quenching! It's perfect for your next summer party! Slightly concentrated, add ice to this lemonade to dilute it when serving. Wonderfully refreshing! Serves 16+)

1 gallon jug of water
2 cups freshly squeezed lemon juice
(or bottled "Real Lemon" juice)
1¾ cups sugar
1/8 tsp salt
16 lbs. of crushed Ice
2 gallon Beverage Dispenser
Optional garnishes: Mint leaves,
4 thinly sliced organic lemons

Directions

1. Remove 2 cups of water from the gallon jug. Pour in lemon juice, sugar, and salt. Secure lid on jug and shake vigorously. Refrigerate. This lemonade mix is slightly concentrated.

2. When ready to serve: Fill a 2 gallon beverage dispenser with 3"of ice. Retrieve the chilled lemonade concentrate and shake the jug a bit to re-mix the contents. Pour concentrate over the ice. The melting ice will dilute the lemonade to taste just right. (Add optional lemon slices and mint leaves to float on top as a pretty garnish, if you'd like.)

3. Next to the serving glasses, it's nice to have additional lemon slices, ice, and straws available for guests to use, if desired. *Delightful!*

Note: For larger groups, prepare several gallon jugs of lemonade concentrate ahead of time. Keep them chilled and ready to refill the dispenser as needed to satisfy your thirsty group.

Homemade Hot Chocolate

(Imagine being in the woods on a cool night, sitting around a warm campfire, talking & laughing and sipping hot chocolate. Mmm-mmmm! Life is good! Makes eight, 8 oz. servings.)

½ gallon whole milk (8 cups)
½ cup sugar
½ cup cocoa powder*
1 cup chocolate chips**
½ tsp vanilla
Optional toppings: mini
marshmallows, whipped cream

Directions
1. In a 3 qt. saucepan, whisk together milk, sugar, and cocoa powder. Cook and stir over medium-low heat until warmed through. Add chocolate chips and stir until chips are melted. (Do not boil.) Stir in vanilla and serve right away.
2. Add optional toppings, as desired. *So good!*   I

Note: To make up a **Dry Hot Chocolate Mix** for camping, whisk together: **2 cups whole milk powder,***** ½ **cup sugar,** ½ **cup cocoa powder, and** ½ **tsp vanilla powder.** Store in an airtight container. Keep **1 cup chocolate chips*** nearby to divide into mugs when reconstituting. (*Use within 6 months*) Serves 8.
To reconstitute 1 serving: Put 1/3 cup dry mix and 2 Tbl chocolate chips into a large mug. Add 1 cup steaming hot water. Stir until chips melt. Add mini marshmallows. *Sip away & enjoy!*

*Hershey's Cocoa 100% Cacao Natural Unsweetened
**We like ½ cup milk chocolate chips + ½ cup semi-sweet chips
***Whole milk powder with real milk (no soy lecithin) tastes best

Hot Apple Cider

(Serve it during cold weather. Hot Cider smells and tastes
wonderful! Makes 1 gallon cider, serving 16 people.)

(2) 64 oz. bottles 100% apple juice
2 organic oranges
2 organic lemons
16 whole cloves
6 cinnamon sticks
¼ tsp salt
½ tsp ground allspice
2/3 cup brown sugar or 2/3 cup pure maple syrup
(Optional) 1 additional cinnamon stick per cup of cider

Directions

1. Wash oranges and lemons. Cut fruit into fourths. Push a whole clove into the **peel** of each fruit section.
2. In a 6 qt. pot, combine apple juice, fruit sections with their cloves in them, cinnamon sticks, salt, allspice, and your choice of sweetener (brown sugar or pure maple syrup). Cover pot with lid. Bring cider mixture to a boil, then reduce temperature to low and simmer for 10 minutes.
3. Just before serving, use a slotted spoon to remove all floating pieces and discard them.
4. Ladle hot cider into mugs. Add an optional cinnamon stick to each mug for a pretty garnish. Serve warm. *Delicious!*

Note: Big kids, teenagers, and adults like spiced cider. However, if you're preparing this drink for little ones, omit the spices and only heat up the 100% apple juice with the brown sugar or pure maple syrup. Serve it slightly warm for toddlers and preschoolers. They'll love it just like that! *Enjoy!*

Raspberry Party Fizz

(A pink raspberry sherbet "float" that is both delicate and refreshing! Perfect for special events and receptions. Serve from a pretty punch bowl. Makes 24, 6 oz. frothy servings.)

1 qt. Raspberry Sherbet
Two, 2 liter bottles of chilled 7-Up or other lemon lime soda
Optional garnish: Whole raspberries, fresh or frozen

Directions
1. Right before serving, place sherbet in punch bowl. Add chilled 7-Up or lemon lime soda.
2. Stir until sherbet is nearly melted. The sherbet will naturally float on top and froth-up. (Optionally, sprinkle a handful of fresh raspberries across the surface.)
3. Ladle into guests' glasses. (This pink drink is particularly lovely when served in transparent glasses or clear plastic cups.) Serve with small beverage napkins—to handle guests' slightly frothy mustaches. *Delightful!*

—MY SPECIAL FAMILY RECIPES —

(Good food links generations. Think of your favorite family foods. Ask your parents and/or grandparents for those favorite food recipes. Record them on the following pages. These recipes will become more precious to you as the years go by!)

Recipe:

Recipe:

Recipe:

Recipe:

"Give me an **I'll**," called out Tim.

"**I'll**," the rest of the Wright cousins called back.

"Give me a **Bake**," Tim called out.

"**Bake!**"

"Give me a **Cookies**," Tim called out.

"**Cookies!**"

"What's that say?"

"**Say!**" called back the rest of the cousins.

"No, you guys got it wrong," said Tim. "You're supposed to say, '**I'll bake cookies!**'"

"What?" said Jonathan.

"**I'll bake cookies**," said Tim.

"Sure, here you go," said Jonathan with a smile, handing Tim a blue apron. "Let us know when they're out of the oven, please."

"Okay," said Tim, "but you guys are taking an awful risk. You know what happened last time."

"What's that?" asked Kimberly.

"The pirates got 'em all," Tim replied.

"Oh, Tim, you and your pirates," said Kimberly.

"Okay," said Tim, "but don't say I didn't warn you. Come on, Robert, matey, let's go bake some cookies."

"Aye, aye, cap'n," Robert replied with a smile.

— WRIGHT FUN! —

Have fun with the Wright Cousins!

- o Top Secret Recipe
- o Food Word Scramble
- o Identify these Wright Cousin Books
- o Wright Cousin Book Titles Scramble
- o Wright Cousin Characters Word Search
- o Nature Scramble
- o Tim Wright Word Scramble
- o Secret Code

Hi, Tim Wright here. How are you doing on your secret mission?

As a reminder, I hid clues to a TOP SECRET RECIPE throughout this book. Did you find all of the gray underlined words identified by the spy hats  and their adjacent gray alphabet LETTERS? Did you get all of the secret words written on the next page?

Hope you enjoy the TOP SECRET RECIPE as much as I do!

— T.W.

— TOP SECRET RECIPE —

(Fill in the Spy Secret Words here)

N ⸺ K ⸺ H ⸺ P ⸺

B ⸺ O ⸺ C ⸺

(Q , stove-top cooking only. Makes 24, 2" C)

½ cup B ⸺
2 cups G ⸺
½ cup M ⸺
4 Tbl A ⸺ D ⸺
½ cup E ⸺ P ⸺ B ⸺
2 tsp L ⸺
3½ cups Q ⸺ O s

Directions

1. In a 3 qt. heavy bottom saucepan, combine B ⸺ ,
   G ⸺ , M ⸺ , & A ⸺ D ⸺ with a W ⸺ spoon
   or silicone S ⸺ . Set pan on stove over medium heat.
   While stirring constantly, bring mixture to a rolling
   I ⸺ and cook for 1 minute. Remove from heat.

2. Add P ⸺ B ⸺ into hot mixture and stir until
   melted and incorporated. Add L ⸺ & O ⸺ s. Stir
   to combine.

3. Drop heaping tablespoons of warm C ⸺ batter
   onto culinary parchment. Cool until set. J ⸺ !

Note: C ⸺ may be stored in a covered container for
up to 1 week or F ⸺ for up to 2 months.

Can You Unscramble These Food Words?

tho ueasc   _____

eeomamhd eic acmer   _____

azpiz   _____

acehp epi   _____

ecrcsten orsll   _____

sakeacpn   _____

tware   _____

salnis   _____

mrbuhaegr   _____

ninoo isgnr   _____

atoc   _____

rorutib   _____

fbee west   _____

tho eohlaocct   _____

cocirlbo   _____

atirsllperac   _____

ntupea etburt acwsidnh _____

Can You Identify these Wright Cousin Books?

Unscramble these Words from the 15 Wright Cousin Book Titles

ltso enmi   _____

nuekns ishp   _____

sdeter epeesrj   _____

eaersrut ayb   _____

ostl tciy   _____

itrgwh sseduigi   _____

mgsinsi sirpsnec   _____

igmnsis pnale   _____

eerstc ntsgea   _____

ftridi ltcaes   _____

tagre aesrunmbi   _____

keta ot het kssei   _____

ylf ginaa   _____

tlrheeesu   _____

hecar rfo eth rasts   _____

nuf boockkoo   _____

Wright Cousin Characters

Find these characters from the Wright Cousin Adventures

```
S  L  A  G  G  M  I  S  S  A  N  N  E  Q  E
M  A  A  C  C  E  B  E  R  J  Y  J  N  K  K
I  R  O  J  E  A  N  N  H  E  G  J  A  Q  A
T  D  N  S  E  E  A  A  U  C  G  J  I  S  T
O  N  E  I  E  T  H  U  T  A  O  A  R  T  R
R  A  A  A  L  A  T  J  R  F  S  U  A  R  I
O  S  L  Y  R  K  A  Y  A  D  O  N  M  A  N
N  E  N  L  E  S  N  M  V  U  M  T  R  U  A
T  L  E  R  H  P  O  A  E  M  I  O  O  N  E
O  L  P  E  T  A  J  R  R  G  K  P  B  S  V
L  A  P  B  U  E  C  K  T  F  G  A  E  E  E
I  I  E  M  S  H  A  E  I  N  N  L  R  E  T
N  R  R  I  E  C  D  V  N  O  E  E  T  F  S
D  A  K  K  P  I  K  S  E  U  Y  D  B  G  I
Y  E  I  L  R  A  H  C  S  S  A  R  I  N  A
```

ALLESANDRA	KREPPEN	SLAGG
AUNT OPAL	LINDY	STEVE
BEN FRANKLIN	MARIAN	STRAUNSEE
CHARLIE	MARK	SUTHERLEE
CHEAPSKATE	MISS ANNE	TIM
EVA	MUDFACE	TORONTO
JAKE	NED	TRAVERTINE
JONATHAN	ONEAL	
JUAN	REBECCA	
KATRINA	ROBERT	
KIMBERLY	SARINA	
KIMOSOGGY	SKIP	

Unscramble these Nature Words

urdstooo

_____

aubilfuet

_____

reuatn

_____

preexlo

_____

nuisatmno

_____

sedert

_____

cvrena

_____

irerv

_____

mesrta

_____

rstee

_____

ysk

_____

insusneh

_____

nwos

_____

inar

_____

eagicrl

_____

seoftr

_____

nweratedru

_____

Unscramble these fun Tim Wright Words

mymmu

ertnosms

ossomieh

troepy

swohm

ecaps enslai

ipreats

ootsiec

eahrsky

eawyeh

oubirtr cpioos

adb gsyu

ceeriodzsap

slaas spcaio

stooracns

hsmu

kyopso

— SECRET CODE —

In 1833, some of author Greg's ancestors crossed the ocean from Hesse Darmstadt to the state of New York in the U.S.A. They were offered land if they would help colonize Colonel Steve Austin's colony in Texas. So they moved on to Texas, which was at that time a colony of Mexico. Author Greg has always wanted to learn more about their immigration and what town they came from in Germany.

Recently, with the help of a guide at the Alamo in San Antonio, Texas, Greg discovered the handwritten signature of one of his ancestors on a real document from 1838. This ancestor signed his name in the Old German Script that he had used in his homeland. A picture of his name is shown below. See if you can decipher it:

(Hint: Use the German Script chart on the next page to figure out the letters and write them on the line above. Notice there are capital and lower case letters.)

Old German Script

You can use the Old German Script like a code. Try writing your own name in German script on the lines below:

— WHAT ABOUT YOU? —

In *The Clue in the Missing Plane*, the Wright cousins visit their friends, the Straunsees, and get to see a lot of their family history in paintings and photos hanging on the inside walls of Alpenhaus. Jonathan is amazed. He realizes he doesn't know that much about his own family.

Learning about family history can be fun and enlightening. What about you? What is your story? You and I may not have royalty in our family lines, but our ancestors were real people. Most of them lived their lives the best they could. They provided for and raised their children and passed on the family legacy.

Our families trace back to many lands all around the world. How about yours? Where did your ancestors live? What kinds of work did they do? Did they have large families or small ones? What are some favorite family stories that have been handed down through your family? Were they sea captains or seamstresses? Carpenters or Cooks? Nurses or farmers? Do you have a special song or lullaby that has been handed down?

On the next few pages, take a few moments to write down some of your favorite memories, family history, and stories.

Where did your ancestors live?

_____
_____
_____
_____
_____
_____
_____
_____
_____
_____
_____

What kinds of work did they do?

_____
_____
_____
_____
_____
_____
_____
_____

How did your parents or grandparents meet?

Ask your oldest living relatives what life was like for them when they were young. Write about it here:

What is a favorite story that has been passed down in your family?

What are some good traits, strengths, talents you and your family are known for?

"Hey Kimberly," said Tim, "can we tell them about our next book?"

"No, it's top secret."

"Wait a minute," said Robert, "we could tell them about the—."

"No, Robert, we've got to keep it a surprise," said Lindy. "You know how word can spread."

"Yes, but it's too much fun," said Tim, "especially when we get to—."

"Not a word," said Kimberly. "This is the end. That part's in our new book."

"Rats," said Tim. "I can't wait to tell them about our next adventure."

"Time to say goodbye," said Jonathan. "Let's all say it together."

"Goodbye everyone!" said all the Wright cousins, waving.

"And, for our next book," added Tim, "don't forget to bring your squirt guns."

"Timothy Wright, you weren't supposed to say that," Kimberly said.

"What?" said Tim, grinning, "we'll need them to be ready."

— INDEX —

Alphabetical Listing of Recipes

— Conversion Charts —

Oven Temperature Equivalents

250°F = 120°C
275°F = 135°C
300°F = 150°C
325°F = 160°C
350°F = 180°C
375°F = 190°C
400°F = 200°C
425°F = 220°C
450°F = 230°C
475°F = 240°C
500°F = 260°C
27,000,000°F = 14,999,982°C (Sun's core temp.)

Measurement Equivalents
(Tbl = Tablespoon, tsp = teaspoon)

$^1/_8$ tsp = 0.5 mL
¼ tsp = 1 mL
½ tsp = 2 mL
1 tsp = 5 mL
1 Tbl = 3 tsp = ½ fluid ounce = 15 mL
2 Tbl = $^1/_8$ cup = 1 fluid ounce = 30 mL
4 Tbl = ¼ cup = 2 fluid ounces = 60 mL
5 $^1/_3$ Tbl = $^1/_3$ cup = 3 fluid ounces = 80 mL
8 Tbl = ½ cup = 4 fluid ounces = 120 mL
10 $^2/_3$ Tbl = $^2/_3$ cup = 5 fluid ounces = 160 mL
12 Tbl = ¾ cup = 6 fluid ounces = 180 mL
16 Tbl = 1 cup = 8 fluid ounces = 240 mL

— List of Useful Kitchen Tools —

Measuring, Mixing, & Processing Tools

☐ Liquid Measuring Cups (Glass): 1 cup, 2 cups, 4 cups
☐ 8-cup glass "batter bowl" with pouring spout, microwave-safe
☐ Dry Measuring Cups Set: ¼ cup, 1/3 cup, ½ cup, 1 cup
☐ Adjustable Measuring Cup, cylinder type for sticky products
☐ Measuring Spoons Set: 1/8 tsp, ¼ tsp, ½ tsp, 1 Tbl
☐ Mixing Bowls: one 2 qts., one 3½ qts.
☐ 1 extra-large stainless steel mixing bowl, 12 qts.
☐ Large fine mesh, stainless steel screen Strainer
☐ Stainless Steel Wire Whisks, 1 large and 1 small
☐ Silicone Spatula
☐ Pizza Roller Cutter
☐ Kitchen Scissors (Kitchen Shears)
☐ Countertop Scraper (stainless steel)
☐ Pastry Brush
☐ Rolling Pin
☐ Apple Peeler Corer
☐ Cookie Cutters
☐ 1½" Cookie Scoop
☐ Pastry Bag with set of frosting tips
☐ Electric Mixer with attachments: whisk, beater, dough hook
☐ Blender

Baking & Stovetop Equipment

☐ Oven Mitts
☐ 2 Cookie Baking Sheets
☐ Cooling racks
☐ Culinary Parchment
☐ Paper Cupcake Liners
☐ Baking Spray
☐ 2 Cake Pans, 9"x13"

- ☐ 2 Loaf Pans, 9" x 5"
- ☐ Jelly Roll Pan with lid, 10"x15"
- ☐ 2 muffin pans, 12 cups each
- ☐ 8" Square Baking Pan, with lid if possible
- ☐ 2 Microwave-safe Mugs, 12 oz. and 24 oz.
- ☐ 3 Metal Pie Pans, 9"
- ☐ 1 glass Pyrex casserole baking dish, wide handles, 2 qt.
- ☐ Broiler Pan
- ☐ 2 Large 15" Pizza Pans
- ☐ Heavy bottom Frying Pan
- ☐ Heavy bottom Stainless Steel Saucepan: either 2 qt. or 3 qt.
- ☐ 6 qt. Heavy bottom Stainless Steel Pot with Glass Lid
- ☐ Wooden Spoon
- ☐ Stainless Steel Ladle
- ☐ Stainless Steel Pancake Turner/Spatula
- ☐ Digital Food Thermometer
- ☐ Wooden Toothpicks

Additional Items

- ☐ 1½ or 2 qt. Ice Cream Maker with Double-Insulated Freezer bowl (like Cuisinart)
- ☐ 2½" Ice Cream Scoop
- ☐ Serrated Bread Knife and Cutting Board
- ☐ Punch Bowl, 2 gallons
- ☐ Beverage Pitchers with lids: ½ gallon, 1 gallon
- ☐ Beverage Dispenser, 2 gallons
- ☐ Plastic Wrap
- ☐ Zip Freezer Bags: Quart and Gallon sizes
- ☐ Aluminum Foil
- ☐ Apron

Please write a review

Authors love hearing from their readers! Please let Greg and Lisa Smith know what you thought about *The Wright Cousin Adventures* #1 *Fun Cookbook: 50 Favorite Desserts You'll Love to Make, Bake, Eat, and Share!* You can contact them at **GregoryOSmith.com**.

Also, please leave a short review on Amazon or your other preferred online store. If you are under age 13, please ask an adult to help you. Your review will help other people to find and enjoy this cookbook.

Thank you!

About the Authors

Greg and Lisa Smith love sharing good things in life with people, including desserts! Teaming up on this cookbook, they've skillfully blended the joy of Lisa's tasty treats with the humor of Greg's fun Wright Cousin characters.

Lisa's decades of cooking experience culminate in this delightful volume. She has carefully streamlined these 50 favorite desserts—including homemade ice cream—to be easy for people to create in their own kitchens. She also took the time to lovingly hand-illustrate each recipe. Lisa hopes these treats will tickle your taste buds and be a joy for you to share with others.

Since 1991, Greg has loved creating wholesome books for children. Each one is full of life, fun, and adventure. This book is no exception. Regarding this, his 19th published book, he says, "There are great tasting, fun experiences ahead for you as you try out these delicious recipes. *Enjoy!*"

Also by award-winning author Gregory O. Smith

The Wright Cousin Adventures series

Join the five Wright Cousins as they explore beautiful pine forested mountains, wide desert expanses, underwater mysteries, tropical island treasures, snow-clad glaciers, and even the wonder and splendor of outer space! This wholesome, action-packed series includes exciting STEM accurate technology and family friendly humor. It is safe to read aloud.

The *Wright Cousin Adventures* series is best enjoyed when read in order, 1-15. This gives a growing experience as the Wright Cousins make new friends, develop their talents, and help people around the world.

 **1 The Treasure of the Lost Mine**—Meet the five Wright cousins in their first big mystery together. I mean, what could be more fun than a treasure hunt with five crazy, daring, ingenious, funny and determined teenagers, right? The adventure grows as the cousins run headlong into vanishing trains, trap doors, haunted gold mines, nefarious crooks, and surprises at every turn!

 **2 Desert Jeepers**—The five Wright cousins are having a blast 4-wheeling in the desert as they look for a long-lost Spanish treasure ship. And who wouldn't? There's so much to see! Palm trees, hidden treasure, UFO's, vanishing stagecoaches, incredible hot sauce, missing pilots. Wait! What?

3 The Secret of the Lost City—A mysterious map holds the key to the location of an ancient treasure city. When the Wright cousins set out on horseback to find it, they run headlong into desert flash floods, treacherous passages, and formidable foes. Saddle up for thrilling discoveries and the cousins' wacky sense of humor in this grand Western adventure!

4 The Case of the Missing Princess—The Wright cousins are helping to restore a stone fort from the American Revolution. They expect hard work, but find more: secret passages, pirates, dangerous waterfalls, a new girl with a fondness for swordplay. This one's a life-changer for Jonathan. Join the Wright Cousins as they try to unravel this puzzling new mystery.

5 Secret Agents Don't Like Broccoli—The spy world will never be the same! Teenage cousins Robert and Tim Wright accidentally become America's top two secret agents—the notorious *Kimosoggy* and *Toronto*. Their mission: rescue the beautiful Princess Katrina Straunsee and the mysterious, all-important Straunsee attaché case. They must not fail, for the future of America is in their hands. Get set for top secret fun and adventure as the Wright cousins try to outsmart the entire spy world. How will they do it?

6 The Great Submarine Adventure—The five Wright cousins have a submarine and they know how to use it! But the deeper they go, the more mysterious Lake Pinecone becomes. Something is wrecking boats on the lake and it's downright scary. How will the Wright cousins uncover the secret before they become the next victims? It's "up periscope" and "man the torpedoes" as the fun-loving Wright cousins dive into this exciting new adventure!

 **7 Take to the Skies**—The five Wright cousins are searching for a missing airplane, but someone keeps sabotaging their efforts. When a sudden lightning storm moves in and the mountains erupt into flames, the cousins must fly into action to help their friends. Will their old World War 2 seaplane hold together through the firestorms?

 **8 The Wright Cousins Fly Again!**—Secret bases, missing airplanes, and an unsolved World War 2 mystery are keeping the Wright cousins busy. As the cousins attempt to raise a long lost airplane from the bottom of Lake Pinecone, they discover a secret lurking deep in the lake that is far more dangerous than they ever expected. Will all their carefully made plans be wrecked?

 **9 Reach for the Stars**—3-2-1-Blastoff! The Wright cousins are out of this world and so is the fun. Join the cousins as they travel into space aboard the new Stellar Spaceplane. Enjoy zero gravity and the incredible views. But what about those space aliens Tim keeps seeing? The Wrights soon discover there really is something out there and it's as dangerous as it is mysterious. The cousins must pull together—with help from family and friends back on earth—if they are ever going to return home to their planet. How will they survive?

10 The Sword of Sutherlee—These are dangerous times in the kingdom of Gütenberg. King Straunsee and his daughters are being held prisoners in their own castle. With secret passages and swords in hand, the cousins must scramble to rescue their friends and the kingdom. How can they do it?

11 The Secret of Trifid Castle—A redirected airline flight leads the Wright cousins back into Gütenberg on a secret mission. Lives hang in the balance as they try out their cool new spy gear. Who can they trust? Join the Wright cousins in this fun, daring, and precarious adventure!

12 The Clue in the Missing Plane— A cold war is about to turn hot in the Kingdom of Gütenberg. Snowstorms, jagged mountains, snowmobiles, enemy soldiers. How will the Wright cousins discover a top secret clue before it's too late?

13 The Wright Disguise—The Wright cousins are back in America and diving into their very busy life of crazy inventions, school classroom mix-ups, and paintball battles. But their visiting friends, princesses Sarina and Katrina, are in danger: Their royal anonymity is compromised by a story gone viral. A treacherous enemy has placed a bounty on their heads. Can the Wright Cousins save their friends before they disappear forever?

14 The Mystery of Treasure Bay—Talofa is a breathtakingly beautiful tropical island located smack dab in the middle of the Wright Cousins' newest itinerary. It has palm trees, lush green mountains, cascading waterfalls, and beautiful lagoons. There is so much to see and do: boogie boarding, scuba diving, exploring, boating, surfing. But danger also lurks in the waters surrounding Talofa.

With fierce storms, sabotage, uncertain friends, and a mysterious lighthouse, how will the Wright Cousins solve this puzzling mystery?

 **15 The Secret of the Sunken Ship—** Anyone up for a dive? This fun and exciting sequel to book #14 finds the Wright cousins searching Talofa and its neighboring tropical islands for a mysterious lost treasure. Along with amazing underwater discoveries, the Wright's and their friends face confusing clues, eerie secret caves, and a desperate gang who will stop at nothing to steal the treasure out from under them. How will the Wright cousins survive the dangers that confront them?

Additional Books by Gregory O. Smith

 **The Hat, George Washington, and Me!** When a mysterious package arrives in the mail with only a tricorn hat and playset inside, 14-year-old Daniel, of course, tries on the hat. Now he's in for it because the hat won't come off! What will his newfound crush Rebecca think of him?
Daniel suddenly finds bullies at every turn, redcoats pounding on the school room door, and a patriot in his cereal box! It's modern-day Millford—a town that is not on the map, any map— and time is running out. How will Daniel and Rebecca solve the mystery of the hat before they're forever trapped in time?

 **Rheebakken 2: Last Stand for Freedom.** "This action-packed novel launches readers directly into the fray on the first page and does not let go until the story's conclusion."—*Riverdancer.* The freedom of the entire world is at stake, and it's up to one man to preserve that freedom—no matter the cost. Fighter pilot Eric Brown has been tasked with the top secret mission of ferrying King Straunsee and his daughter Allesandra to safety in the United States. Unfortunately, there are many others who would choose to see the monarch destroyed rather than permitting him to secure global freedom.

This is a fast-paced, action-centered story that will appeal to teen and young adult readers who appreciate military stories with a wholesome approach.

 **Strength of the Mountains**—An award-winning story of courage, faith, family, and friendship. "Loved it! Awesome adventure on survival and a bit of romance."

"You're kidding, right? Balloon camping? That's what you want for your graduation present?" The morning arrives. The balloon is filled. An unexpected storm strikes. Matt, all alone, is swept off into the wilderness in an unfinished balloon. How will he survive? Will he ever make it home again?

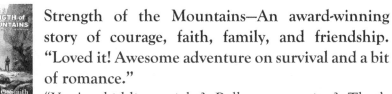 *Wright Cousin Adventures #1 Fun Cookbook ~ 50 Favorite Desserts You'll Love to Make, Bake, Eat, and Share!* Each delicious dessert recipe includes easy-to-follow directions and author Lisa's helpful and unique, *hand-drawn illustrations.* You'll also find classic Wright Cousin humor, puzzles, secret codes, *and* clues to Tim Wright's "Top Secret Recipe" hidden somewhere inside the cookbook.

LISA A. SMITH & GREGORY O. SMITH

Please tell your family and friends about these fun and exciting new adventures so they can enjoy them too! Help spread the word!

https://gregoryosmith.com/

Made in the USA
Las Vegas, NV
01 November 2023